CALLED
UP YONDER

CALLED
UP YONDER

Glimpsing the Journey
Into the Beyond

KATHARINE WINTER, CHM

Library of Congress Control Number: 2016958732

ISBN-13: 978-0-990887782

Pocamug Press
Maysville, KY
www.pocamug.com

To all the Earth angels who provide care and a loving presence for those making their transition

About the lotus flower:

"As something that is associated with rebirth, it is no surprise that the lotus flower is also associated with death, and the famous Egyptian book of the dead is known to include spells that are able to transform a person into a lotus, thus allowing for resurrection. In Hinduism the lotus flower is associated with beauty, fertility, prosperity, spirituality, and eternity. In Buddhism the lotus is seen as a sign of rebirth, but additionally it is associated with purity."

Dean Ravenscroft

https://www.lotusflowermeaning.net/

Preface

When my father was dying in 1999, no one explained to the family what was happening and I didn't come to the understanding or realization he was dying until the very end. He had suffered a minor stroke, was in the hospital and apparently doing well, but a day later had a second stroke and fell into a coma, remaining so, until he died in the hospital approximately one week later. This frustrating experience left me with the awareness of how poorly the medical establishment handled both my father's condition and communication with the family. Basically the technique used was avoidance. I was left with especially wanting to know more about the process of dying and its symptoms in particular, but could not find the answers I was seeking.

Now I understand from his breathing patterns and congestion (sometimes referred to as the death rattle) that he was actively dying, or saying it in another way, he was laboring to leave this world. I strongly regret being so ill prepared with knowledge and information about what was taking place. But now that I understand, in my mind's eye I see my father smiling at me and giving me the thumbs up sign....and who's to say this "communication" isn't for real?!

Acknowledgments

A huge heartfelt thank you is due Lynda Kuckenbrod, founder of Therapy Harp Training Program LLC and the Hearts in Harmony Project, for affording me the prospect to explore and write about the topic in this publication. This learning process has been an enriching experience that might not have happened without the provision of this opportunity. I am enormously grateful to you, Lynda!

Special thanks goes to my family members for all their help in preparing this publication—especially to Kate for suggesting it be published, to Sarah for her excellent judgement in editing recommendations, to my husband Bill for his support, and to Michael at Pocamug Press.

Why Discuss the Journey?

A variety of different words and expressions are used when talking about life's end; but whatever terminology is used, death is an inescapable fact of life. Yet in our present culture it seems we do all we can to avoid accepting this inevitable truth. Continually evading this topic leaves us poorly prepared when it comes time to face the death of loved ones or even our own mortality.

Until it strikes close to home, death may not even seem real to us but is just what happens to other people. American author William Saroyan rather humorously illustrated this concept in a quote made just days before he died, "Everybody has got to die, but I have always believed an exception would be made in my case. Now what?"

Our cultural attitude of avoidance extends into the medical profession where death may be viewed as a failure rather than a natural part of life. There appears to be a lot of confusion over what to do for a seriously ill patient, throwing families into turmoil and sometimes putting members at odds with one another. Patients may be kept alive on life support against their wishes. I have also seen cases where a patient of advanced age who had been otherwise healthy, was abandoned by the medical establishment when more could have been done to help the patient, and more could have been done to help the family understand what was happening to their family member. Not only were they all basically left out in the cold, but some of the medical staff were particularly unsympathetic to the point of hostility— seemingly angry that they should have to explain anything or even be bothered with the family of a dying patient.

I began exploring the topic of the journey into the beyond during my certification process for becoming a healthcare musician. Responsibilities of a healthcare musician often include playing for both the terminally ill and the actively dying. I wanted to be more at ease with the topic of dying so that I could better serve those in need.

My purpose in writing this publication is to introduce a broader perspective than what our culture generally offers on this subject, but especially to acquaint the reader with additional reading where more in-depth information can be found. There are insights to be gained from those who have worked closely with the dying and who share their knowledge to benefit both the dying and the bereaved. Most of us know very little about the process of dying. We don't know what to expect when a person is dying and we are unacquainted with the signs and symptoms. Since the prognosis of death for each of us is 100% it only makes sense to learn a little about the process instead of ignoring and avoiding the topic.

"It sounds paradoxical: by excluding death from our life we cannot live a full life, and by admitting death into our life we enlarge and enrich it."

Etty Hillesum

Is There Life After Death?

Many people in our culture hold firmly to the belief that there is no afterlife— you live, you die and that's the end. This position views death as the ultimate destruction. Some in this group have stated that belief in an afterlife is mere fantasy— nothing more than wishful thinking. To these people there is little evidence that will be accepted as support in belief of an afterlife.

Many others firmly believe in life after death— that consciousness survives death. This position views death not as an end but as a transition from one realm to another. Sometimes this belief is a matter of faith but other members of this group have had near-death experiences (NDEs) and hold this as proof.

There are numerous books written on the topic of NDEs by people who have had these occurrences which they consider a glimpse into the afterlife.

Author Raymond Moody MD, in his classic publication *Life After Life* reports on NDEs and the various elements that may be experienced. In the book's introduction, Dr. Moody states he is not trying to prove there is life after death, nor does he think that proof is currently possible. He himself has not had a near-death experience. His purpose is to "draw attention to a phenomenon which is at once very widespread and very well hidden, and, at the same time, help create a more receptive public attitude toward it."

Some examples of NDE components that he found include many hearing they are pronounced dead, incidences of auditory sensations, sensations of being pulled rapidly through a tunnel or dark space, an encounter with a very bright light, a life review, and meeting spiritual presences who apparently were there to ease their transition or tell them their time to die had not come. He notes that not all components happen to each person. Many who have NDEs have difficulty articulating their experience, saying there are no words in our language to describe it.

In this same book, Dr. Moody points out parallels between the NDE reports he has gathered and descriptions in the works of Plato, the Bible, The Tibetan Book of the Dead, and the writings of Swedish scientist, philosopher and theologian, Emanuel Swedenborg.

There have also been research studies on this topic in which similarities of experiences have been found— even among differing cultures and belief systems.

The book *At The Hour of Death* is devoted entirely to research comparing the observations by medical personnel of dying patients living in the U.S. (largely Christian) with those in India (largely Hindu). Over 1,000 deathbed observations were reported by doctors and nurses in both countries. The study found that patient experiences in both countries were remarkably similar, differing mainly in the religious figure the patients said they saw as a presence in the room.

An especially notable book on NDEs is *Proof of Heaven*, written by respected neurosurgeon, Eben Alexander, MD. He was very much steeped in the tradition of scientific medical academia and the idea of physical death being the end of life... until he himself had the near-death experience that became the focus of his book. Prior to his experience he did not believe in heaven, God, or the soul, and believed that NDEs were nothing more than fantasies.

In the appendix his attending physician gives a statement confirming Dr. Alexander's medical diagnosis and treatment. Also in the appendix Dr. Alexander considers some neuroscientific hypotheses that have been put forth to try and explain his NDE and then he writes why each hypothesis fails in this regard. He now believes "that true health can be achieved only when we realize that God and the soul are real and that death is not the end of personal existence but only a transition."

The Process of Dying

*"You see we are all dying. It's only a matter of time.
Some of us just die sooner than others."*

Dudjom Rinpoche

Death has been described as a birth into the next life. Just as there are phases that accompany and are involved with the birthing process, there are also stages that accompany the dying process. Just as in childbirth, the stages are somewhat flexible and may not follow a strict pattern. Each person is unique. These stages apply to a person in the process of dying and may not apply in the case of a sudden unexpected death.

As an end of life educator, Barbara Karnes RN, author of *The Eleventh Hour: A Caring Guideline for the Hours to Minutes Before Death* provides a guide for those close to the dying by explaining what is happening and even giving suggestions (and thereby letting the family know it's okay to do these things) on what they might do that they might not have thought about otherwise, both during the time the patient is dying and afterward.

An example she provides is that after the patient has died, the family might give a final bath by gently wiping down the body with a wet cloth using water to which a few drops of essential oil or the dead person's favorite cologne has been added. Candles may be lighted and prayers said to make this a sacred ritual. If the death has occurred at home, once the body has been removed, a memento such as a flower, rosary, bible, stuffed animal, etc. could be placed on the pillow of the newly made bed. These small acts of love can be both a tribute to the deceased and a comfort to the bereaved.

Author and thanatologist David Kessler compares dying to "...shutting down a large factory filled with engines and assembly lines and giant boilers. Everything does not suddenly go quiet when the 'off' switch is pushed. Instead, the machinery creaks and moans as it slows to a halt." He continues, "The separation of body and soul looks painful to us, the survivors, (as) the body moans and creaks but internally it is at peace."

In his book *Needs of the Dying: A Guide for Bringing Hope, Comfort, and Love to Life's Final Chapter*, Mr. Kessler devotes a chapter "What Death Looks Like" to describing what survivors might "see, hear, feel and smell" as someone dies. These may involve changes to sleeping and eating patterns, incontinence, restlessness, cyanosis (a bluish tint of the skin due to lack of oxygen in the blood), fever, foaming at the mouth, and breathing changes, including the "death rattle" which is a result of the body's inability to clear secretions collecting in the upper airways. If necrotic tissue is present there will likely be an odor. Sometimes the dying person may "let out a loud yell" which is attributed not to pain but to "undergoing a physical spasm involving the voice box and lungs in their final protest against the separation of body and soul."

Mr. Kessler's intent was that this clear and straightforward description of the dying process, often a taboo topic, could benefit others. Barbara Karnes also provides an excellent summary of the dying process in her booklet *Gone From My Sight: The Dying Experience*.

As Ms. Karnes says, "We go through labor to enter this world and labor to leave it. Some labors are short, some long. During both labors, our family and friends support and guide us up to the time of delivery. In both cases, the person who is birthing or dying is doing the majority of the work."

In childbirth, relaxation eases the birth; in the dying person, relaxation eases the transition. Stated in *The Eleventh Hour*: "Tension creates a tightness that locks us in our body and makes our labor longer. Relax and we can release easily."

A word about hospice seems appropriate here. The term "hospice" was originally used to describe a place of shelter and rest for weary travelers. In 1967 the term was used in specialized care for the dying at St. Christopher's Hospice in a suburb of London. In hospice care, emphasis is on quality of life rather than length of life. This means management of pain and other symptoms.

Hospice care involves a team-oriented approach of medical care, pain management, and emotional and spiritual support tailored to the patient's wishes. Emotional and spiritual support is also extended to the family and loved ones. Generally, this care is provided in the patient's home or in a home-like setting operated by a hospice program.

In the book *Final Gifts: Understanding the Special Awareness, Needs, and Communications of the Dying*, authors Maggie Callanan and Patricia Kelley tell what they have learned in twenty years of working as hospice nurses. I have heard many of the same stories from local hospice staff. The authors saw similar patterns of what they called "near death awareness" in communications of dying patients regardless of illness, culture, gender, age, ethnicity, and religious background.

Many patients described what they were experiencing as follows: being in the presence of someone not alive, the need to prepare for travel or a change, mention of a place they alone could see, or their knowledge of when death would occur.

People who are dying are often more aware of that fact than the people around them realize— even having an idea when they will die and giving clues in their speech. But frequently the messages are subtle and easily overlooked because the language used is symbolic. In these cases family members may interpret the messages as confusion and dismiss them. This results in missed opportunities to prepare for the loss and best use the time that is left. It's not known why some dying people use subtle symbolic language rather than simply say, "I'm dying on this particular day or at this exact time." Perhaps it's an unconscious rather than a conscious awareness of death that drives this form of communication.

Frequently, dying people will see presences in the room that others cannot see. The presences are often identified as close friends, family members or a religious figure, all who have already died. This is commonly misinterpreted as hallucinations induced by medications, which can lead well-meaning onlookers to suggest changes in a patient's medicine regimen— changes which are likely unnecessary and which may cause the patient much suffering. Some terminally ill have the experience of seeing presences months before their deaths while with others it happens very close to their time of death.

Those who work with hospice and have been present at numerous deaths explain that none of us die alone— we are accompanied by those who have died before us or some spiritual being(s), although these presences may be seen only by those dying.

Some situations may happen that are of great concern to the living, causing feelings of unresolved guilt with regard to their loved one's passing. One situation is when the caregiver briefly leaves the dying person, who has been in bed and too weak to move. Upon return the patient is found lifeless on the floor. It appears that the patient tried to get out of bed, fell and the resulting fall caused the death. The caregiver blames himself and believes this wouldn't have happened had the caregiver remained with the patient. This situation is described by the authors in *Final Gifts*, who explain "Just before they die, and usually without warning, some patients can muster an unusual strength." An alternate possibility the authors suggest is that the patient was attempting to go towards something they saw when they died; death was not caused by the fall.

A difficult choice often comes when the family must make the decision to continue certain forms of life support. Each case is unique and should be considered on an individual basis. Hospice chaplain Reverend Hank Dunn in *Hard Choices for Loving People* reminds us that the permanent inability to take in food or water is a terminal condition. Removing a feeding tube does not kill the patient, the underlying condition that caused the inability does.

The Needs of the Dying

"Death... is not the ultimate tragedy. The ultimate tragedy is depersonalization... dying in an alien and sterile arena, separated from the spiritual nourishment that comes from being able to reach out to a loving hand."

Norman Cousins

Elisabeth Kübler-Ross's work focused our attention upon the dying and bringing into our awareness the dying process and the needs of the dying. David Kessler continued her work and identified needs of the dying in his book *Needs of the Dying; A Guide for Bringing Hope, Comfort, and Love to Life's Final Chapter*.

The first and most fundamental need he lists is "The need to be treated as a living human being." Another is "To die in peace and dignity." In simple summary the needs of the dying mirror the needs of the living. If we already understood and practiced this, a book would not have needed to be written!

Even when a dying person appears to be nonresponsive, it is believed and largely accepted by the medical community that the auditory function remains intact and is the last sense to go. Therefore it is important to continue to communicate with a nonresponsive dying person when providing services (such as bathing or turning the patient over, etc.) and not speak about him as if he were not there. Even when those who are dying appear to not be present they are still human beings with human needs and deserve to be treated with dignity and respect, the same as the living.

People generally die as they live. Some prefer to have loved ones with them as they die while others prefer to die alone, even waiting for friends or family members to leave before they make their transition.

Sometimes something or someone is needed so death can be peaceful, such as the desire to reconcile personal, spiritual or moral relationships, and/or requests to remove some barrier to achieving this peace. According to the authors of *Final Gifts* the underlying issues tend to be around relationships— whether with other people, a supreme being, or with themselves.

Sometimes the request is clear, for example, saying they want to speak with someone to reconcile a relationship. Other times the request is not clear and may be missed, or interpreted as unimportant or as confusion. If the patient cannot communicate his needs he may become agitated. If the issue is unresolved patients may appear to die in pain which may be emotional or spiritual rather than physical. Some patients may even delay the timing of their death.

Conclusion

"...life is nothing but a continuing dance of birth and death, a dance of change. Learning to live is learning to let go."

Sogyal Rinpoche

In a world where sex, youth and power reign supreme, death is the frightening enemy to be avoided and from which to escape. Those of advanced age, perhaps because they are seen as drawing closer to death and are a reminder of our mortality, are also pushed aside and even shunned. Herein lies an opportunity for us to bring beauty and connection to those very much in need of it. In this process, both the elderly and the dying are afforded dignity and affirmed as the whole people that they are.

For the unafraid and faithful, death will no longer be that unexplored forbidden room with imagined dark secrets. As the door to the room is opened and the light shined in, it becomes a room as any other, a part of life no longer hidden away in fear but overflowing with love.

Bibliography and Further Reading

Alexander, Eben. *Proof of Heaven: A Neurosurgeon's Journey into the Afterlife*. New York, NY: Simon & Schuster, 2012. http://www.eternea.org

Aries, Philippe. *The Hour of Our Death: The Classic History of Western Attitudes Toward Death Over the Last One Thousand Years*. New York, NY: Vintage Books, 2008

Aries, Philippe. *Western Attitudes Toward Death from the Middle Ages to the Present (The Johns Hopkins Symposia in Comparative History)*. Baltimore, MD: Johns Hopkins University Press, 1975.

Burke, John. *Imagine Heaven*. Grand Rapids, MI: Baker Books, 2025.

Burpo, Todd & Sonja. *Heaven Changes Everything: The Rest of the Story*. Nashville, TN: Thomas Nelson, 2015.

Callanan, Maggie and Patricia Kelley. *Final Gifts: Understanding the Special Awareness, Needs, and Communications of the Dying*. New York, NY: Simon & Schuster, 2012.

Cole, Jeffrey. *Returning Home*. Victoria, BC: Trafford Publishing, 2006.

Dunn, Hank. *Hard Choices for Loving People*. Naples, FL: Quality of Life Publishing Company, 2016.

Eadie, Betty J. & Curtis Taylor. *Embraced by the Light*. U.S. and Canada: Bantam Books,1994.

Gawande, Atul. *Being Mortal*. New York, NY: Henry Holt and Company, 2014.

Harris, Trudy. *Glimpses of Heaven*. Grand Rapids, MI: Revell, 2017.

Hospice Foundation of America. https:// hospicefoundation.org

Johnson, Judith. *Making Peace with Death and Dying: A Practical Guide to Liberating Ourselves from the Death Taboo*. New York, NY: Monkfish Book Publishing Company, 2022.

Karnes, Barbara. End of Life Educational Materials for Families & Professionals. https:// bkbooks.com.

Kellehear, Allan. *Visitors at the End of Life: Finding Meaning and Purpose in Near-Death Phenomena*. New York, NY: Columbia University Press, 2020.

Kellehear, Allan. *A Social History of Dying*. Cambridge, UK: Cambridge University Press, 2007.

Kessler, David. *The Needs of the Dying: A Guide for Bringing Hope, Comfort, and Love to Life's Final Chapter*. New York, NY: HarperCollins, 2007.

Kübler-Ross, Elisabeth. *Death: The Final Stage of Growth*. New York, NY: Simon & Schuster, 1997.

Kübler-Ross, Elisabeth. *On Life After Death, revised*. Berkley, CA: Celestial Arts, 2008.

McFadden, Julie, RN. *Nothing to Fear: Demystifying Death to Live More Fully*. New York, NY: TarcherPerigee, 2024.

McVea, Crystal. *Waking Up in Heaven*. New York, NY: Howard Books, 2013.

Moody, Raymond A. *Life After Life*. San Francisco, CA: HarperOne, 2015.

Moorjani, Anita. *Dying To Be Me: My Journey from Cancer, to Near Death, to True Healing*. Vista, CA: Hay House Publishing, 2012. https://www.anitamoorjani.com/my-nde

Osis, Karlis and Erlendur Haraldsson. *At The Hour of Death*. Guilford, Surrey, UK: White Crow Books, 2012.

Piper, Don and Cecil Murphey. *90 Minutes in Heaven: A True Story of Life and Death*. Grand Rapids, MI: Revell, 2014.

Rinpoche, Sogyal. *The Tibetan Book of Living and Dying*. New York, NY: HarperOne, 2020.

Siegel, Bernie S. Love, *Medicine & Miracles*. New York, NY: HarperPerennial, 1990.

Notes